Rookie reader

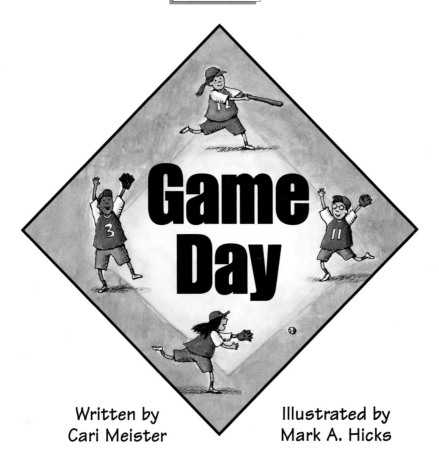

Game Day

Written by
Cari Meister

Illustrated by
Mark A. Hicks

Children's Press®
A Division of Scholastic Inc.
New York • Toronto • London • Auckland • Sydney
Mexico City • New Delhi • Hong Kong
Danbury, Connecticut

For my dad—a great coach!
—C.M.

For Kade K.
—M.A.H.

Reading Consultant
Katharine A. Kane
Education Consultant
(Retired, San Diego County Office of Education
and San Diego State University)

Library of Congress Cataloging-in-Publication Data
Meister, Cari.
Game day / written by Cari Meister ; illustrated by Mark A. Hicks.
    p. cm. — (Rookie reader)
Summary: Illustrations and simple text describe the events of a baseball
game.
    ISBN 0-516-22262-7 (lib. bdg.)   0-516-25964-4 (pbk.)
    [1. Baseball—Fiction.] I. Hicks, Mark A., ill. II. Title. III. Series.
    PZ7.M515916 Gam 2001
    [E]—dc21

                                    00-047368

A shirt.
A glove.
A hat.

3

Two teams.
A ball.
A bat.

5

The hit.

The run.

The slide.

9

The throw.

The catch.

Game's tied!

The hit.

The miss.

The run.

The throw!

He's safe!

We won!

Word List (23 words)

a	hat	teams
ball	he's	the
bat	hit	throw
catch	miss	tied
day	run	two
game	safe	we
game's	shirt	won
glove	slide	

About the Author

Cari Meister lives on a small farm in Minnesota with her husband John, her son Edwin, their dog Samson, two horses, three cats, two pigs, and two goats. She is the author of more than twenty books for children, including *I Love Rocks* (also a *Rookie Reader*), *When Tiny was Tiny*, and *Busy, Busy City Street* (both from Viking).

About the Illustrator

Mark A. Hicks has created award-winning artwork for books, magazines, and paper products.

10-04

ER   Meister, Cari
      Game day.

GAYLORD RG